A Giant First-Start Reader

This easy reader contains only 43 different words, repeated often to help the young reader develop word recognition and interest in reading.

Basic word list for *The Spelling Bee*

a	he	spell
am	help	spelled
and	honey	spelling
are	hum	the
bee	I	these
bees	is	they
busy	lazy	think
buzz	learning	this
can	making	to
day	needed	too
do	needs	who
get	not	words
guess	one	work
hard	said	works
	so	

The Spelling Bee

Written by Sharon Gordon

Illustrated by Tom Garcia

Troll Associates

Library of Congress Cataloging in Publication Data

Gordon, Sharon.
    The spelling bee.

    Summary: The spelling bee demonstrates the importance
of knowing how to spell.
    [1. English language—Spelling—Fiction.   2. Bees—
Fiction]   I. Garcia, Tom.   II. Title.
PZ7.G65936Sp   [E]   81-4648
ISBN 0-89375-535-4 (case)   AACR2
ISBN 0-89375-536-2 (pbk.)

Buzz! Hum!

These bees are busy.

They work hard.

They are busy making honey.

Work . . . work . . . work.

This bee is busy, too.

He works hard, too.

He is busy making words.

He is learning to spell.

Words . . . words . . . words.

The busy bees do not think he is busy.

They think he is lazy.

"Buzz! Hum!"

"Who needs a spelling bee?"

"I am learning to spell," said the spelling bee.

"I can spell 'busy' and 'bees'."

"And I can spell 'help'," said the spelling bee.

"Buzz! Hum! Who needs a spelling bee?"

One day, the busy bees needed help.

"Help!" said the busy bees.

"I can get help," said the spelling bee.

"I can spell 'help'."

So the spelling bee spelled "help."

He spelled, "Help the busy bees."

Who needs a spelling bee?

The busy bees do!

Who is learning to spell?

Guess who!